The Gymkhana
WOODLEY FARM
The road was blocked here
Road to the Fire Station
The Town
RIVER
Where the fire was
The green parcel was dropped here
Hyde Heath
THE FINISH OF THE RALLY

7
4
2
HO

GUMDROP ON THE RALLY

Story and pictures by Val Biro

WHSMITH
EXCLUSIVE
· BOOKS ·

THERE WAS A STRANGE SIGHT at the Red Lion one sunny morning in June. The vintage cars had come to start their big Rally of the year. Never was there such a collection of fine old cars in the yard. Each had a Rally number fixed to it.

Number 1 was an Alvis Duck-Back, and Number 2 a Morris Bullnose. The Model-T Ford was Number 3, the Speed-Six Bentley 4. Number 5 was a two-seater Dodge, and Number 6 was an Alfa-Romeo. The small Humber was Number 7, and the big Renault was 8.

And then there was a blue car, with a black hood and a brass horn. It was Number 9: an Austin Clifton Heavy Twelve-Four, vintage 1926, driven by Bill McArran. It was Gumdrop.

Bill's wife, Sally, was there too, to be Gumdrop's navigator and to show Bill the way on the Rally.

GHRAUPP! went the organizer's klaxon. Everyone was silent. "You will follow the instructions," he said, "and watch out for signposts. Make sure that you stay on the right road. If you don't you'll lose marks. Cars will start at one-minute intervals, drive for sixty miles and finish at Hyde Heath. The first car to arrive at four o'clock will be the winner. And don't get lost!"

HONK-HONK! went Gumdrop's horn, when at last it was his turn to start. Bill drove for ten miles, carefully following the right road according to the instructions that Sally read out. Then they came to a cross-roads. "Which way now?" asked Bill.

"Thataway!" shouted a young man by the roadside.

"Thanks!" said Bill, and drove down a bumpy road. It twisted and it turned. It was steep and it was narrow. It turned again and then, by a gate, it stopped.

"This *can't* be the way," Sally said.

"That chap back there must have fooled us," said Bill. "We must turn round now, and look for the right road."

TOOTLE-TOOT! went a little horn. Bill stopped Gumdrop. There, in the road, was a small boy in a pedal car. He was crying. "I'm tired," he said. "And I think I'm lost. My name is Peter and I live at Mapletree Farm."

"That's the farm down the road," said Sally. "I noticed the name as we went past."

"Right," said Bill to the small boy, "we'll put your car in Gumdrop and take you home."

MOOO! went the cows at Mapletree Farm when they saw Peter again, and the donkey said EEYAAW. The farmer was also glad to see Peter back, and to show how pleased he was he gave Bill a can of oil for Gumdrop and asked if they would have a cup of coffee.

"Thank you very much," said Bill, "but we can't stay.
We must turn round now and look for the right road."

They turned left,
and they turned right,
and they drove for miles, searching.
Then they heard a loud NEEEEIGH!
It was a pony in a trailer.
"Our car broke down," said the little
girl in jodhpurs, "and we must get to
the gymkhana in time for the
jumping competition. Could
you please take us?"

"Jump in!" said Bill. "We'll hitch the trailer to Gumdrop and get you to the show in time."

And they did get there in time,
just as the starting bell went CLANG!
Soon it was the little girl's turn to ride
round. Her pony jumped so well
that they won a rosette.

"You have been very kind," said the girl's father to Bill and Sally, and to show how pleased he was he gave them a set of sparking-plugs for Gumdrop and asked them if they would like to stay and see some more jumping.

"Thank you very much," said Bill, "but we must turn round now and look for the right road."

This time they turned right,
and then left, and drove on
for miles, searching.
They found themselves in a town,
where all the bells were going
DING-DONG-DOINNG!

The streets were crowded and there were strange vehicles driving slowly along. It was a carnival procession. There was no room to turn, so Gumdrop had to drive slowly along with them.

Just then a man ran up to Gumdrop. "Please do us the favour, Sir, of conveying His Worship the Mayor to the Town Hall in your exquisite vehicle. His official car has unfortunately developed a puncture."

"My word, it is a pleasure to ride in an original Twelve-Four again," said the Mayor. "I had just such a car myself when I was young," he said. And they drove along the cheering crowds.

"My grateful thanks to you both," said the Mayor when they reached the Town Hall. And to show how pleased he was, he gave Bill his old authentic Heavy Twelve-Four instruction book and driving manual for Gumdrop, and asked them if they would stay for lunch.

"Thank you very much," said Bill, "but we must turn round now and look for the right road."

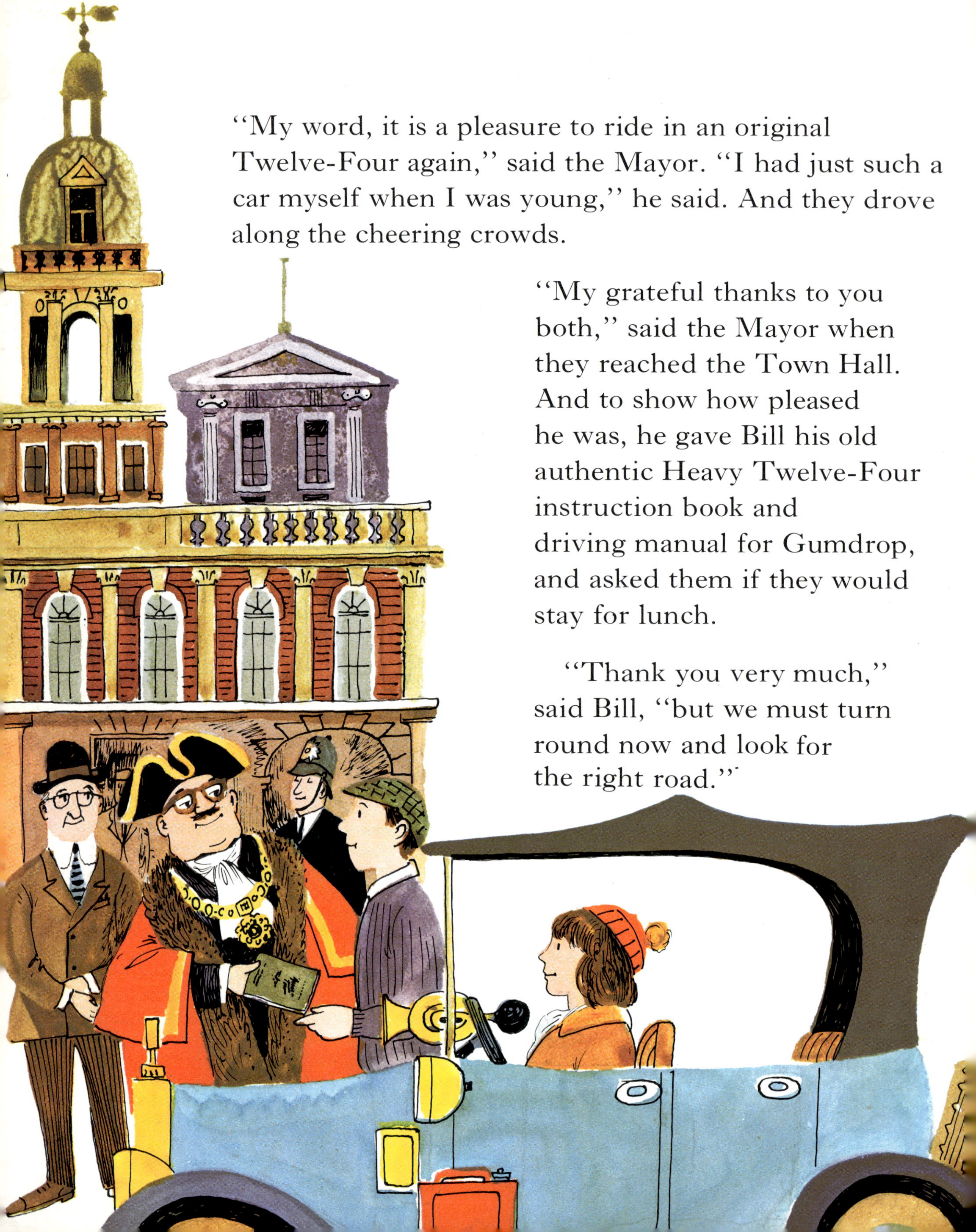

They turned left,
and then right,
and out of the town.
They drove on for
miles, searching.
Then they stopped.

The road was blocked by a tractor. "Please help!" cried the driver, Mr. Woodley. "I was on my way to market, but the door of my trailer burst open and all the piglets got away! They must have scampered back to my farm."

Mr. Woodley got into the back seat of Gumdrop, and they drove after the piglets.

Mr. Woodley found four piglets in a pond.

Sally found three in the shed.

Bill found two in the bath tub.

And the last one was in a barrel.

They put them all into Gumdrop and took them back to the trailer. The piglets went SQUEEEEEK-SQUEEEEK!

"Thank you for rounding them up," said Mr. Woodley. And to show how pleased he was, he gave Bill a set of vintage tools for Gumdrop, which were in his tractor.

"Thank you very much," said Bill. "We must turn round now and look for the right road."

It was getting late now. They turned right, then left, then right again, still searching for the right road. Then, at a cross-roads they saw a signpost. It was pointing to Hyde Heath, where the Rally was to finish. "We've found the right road at last," said Sally to Bill.

Just then, they heard a CRACKLE, SIZZLE, CRACKLE and saw a cloud of black smoke. "That hayrick's on fire!" cried Bill, "and there's nobody at the farm!"

There was only one thing to do.
Bill turned Gumdrop round again and
drove back to the town to call the fire-brigade.

CLANG-CLANG, CLANG-CLANG! went the fire-engine, and HONK-HONK! went Gumdrop, as he led the firemen back to the blaze. The hayrick was burning furiously, but the buildings were still unharmed. The firemen unrolled the hoses and put the fire out in no time.

Just then the owner of the farm returned, and to show how pleased he was, he gave Bill a genuine vintage two-gallon petrol tin for Gumdrop.
"Thank you very much," said Bill.
Then he turned to Sally. "We really must go on now and finish the Rally."

9
PR 6719
BAD 783

They drove on for two miles, when they heard a GR-GRRRRHHR, getting louder. A motor-bike came roaring towards them. It had to brake hard when it saw Gumdrop—SCREEEEECH!—it swerved left, it lurched right, it skidded left again, and it dropped a parcel from the back.

But it didn't crash, and it didn't stop. With an alarmed glance at Gumdrop, the rider kicked down a gear, accelerated fast and roared away.

"It's that chap with the long hair again!" cried Bill. "The one who fooled us this morning. And look! He dropped his parcel!"

By this time the motor-bike was long out of sight. So Bill picked up the parcel and put it on the back seat. Then they drove on to the Rally.

The other cars were already there when they arrived. Gumdrop was last, because Bill and Sally had not found the right road.

GHRAUPP-GHRAUPP! went the organizer's klaxon. "Ladies and gentlemen," he announced, "the Rally is now over, but we can't give out the prizes because they've been stolen!"

"Stolen!" cried Bill. Then he remembered the parcel. He got it out and opened it. And there, sure enough, were the three shiny silver cups!

"Wonderful!" cried the organizer. "The thief has been foiled, and we can award the prizes after all. And though Gumdrop hasn't won a silver cup, I give him this brass starting-handle as a special prize for solving the crime!"

Everyone cheered, and all the cars sounded their horns: GLUUURK-GUG and BLEEP-BLIP; HONK-TONK and TOOTLE-TOOT!

So that was the end of the Rally. Gumdrop was the last car, but everybody cheered him. He didn't find the right road, but he helped a lost little boy,

a girl with a pony,  a mayor in a procession, 

and a farmer with ten little pigs.

He also helped to put out a fire, and he found the silver cups. He didn't win a cup himself, but just the same he was given

a can of oil,  a set of sparking-plugs, 

an authentic Twelve-Four instruction book and driving

manual, 

a set of vintage tools, 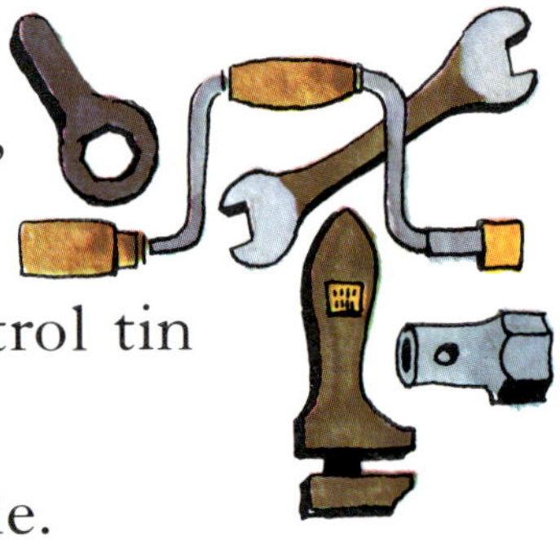

 a genuine vintage two-gallon petrol tin

and a brass  starting-handle.

Gumdrop was the happiest vintage car on the Rally.

Gumdrop on the Rally

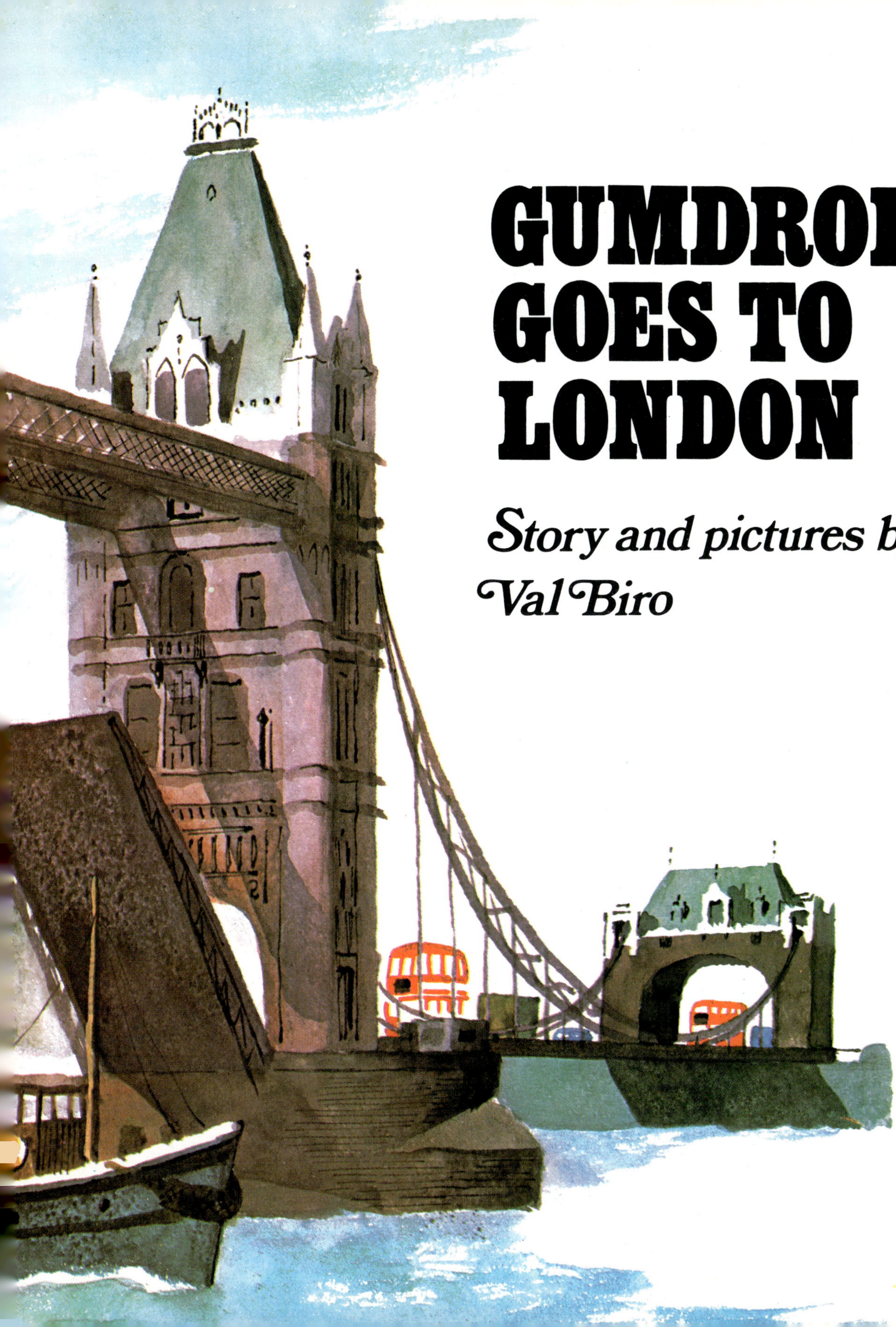

GUMDROP GOES TO LONDON

Story and pictures by

Val Biro

MR JOSIAH OLDCASTLE lived in a small house in the country and he liked it very much.
He had a small garden which he liked even more.
There was also a small garage with large red doors and inside the garage was something which Mr Oldcastle liked best of all.
It was a blue car with a black hood and a brass horn; it had four large wheels and
four small lamps and a brass thermometer. It was an Austin Clifton Heavy Twelve-Four, vintage 1926, and it was called Gumdrop.

One fine morning
a letter arrived. "It is from
BBC Television in London,"
cried Mr Oldcastle, "and they want
Gumdrop to appear on a programme
tomorrow afternoon at three o'clock!"
Mr Oldcastle was delighted. "Millions of people
will see Gumdrop," he thought, "so I had better
polish him up until he shines."
And he did just that.

The sun was shining when he set out next morning, so Mr Oldcastle put Gumdrop's hood down. At a quarter to twelve they crossed Tower Bridge and drove past the Tower of London.

Suddenly a Yeoman of the Guard came hurrying towards them. "My name is Biffin, Sir, and I would be much obliged for a lift to Westminster. I can't go by bus, because they won't let this partisan of mine on board."

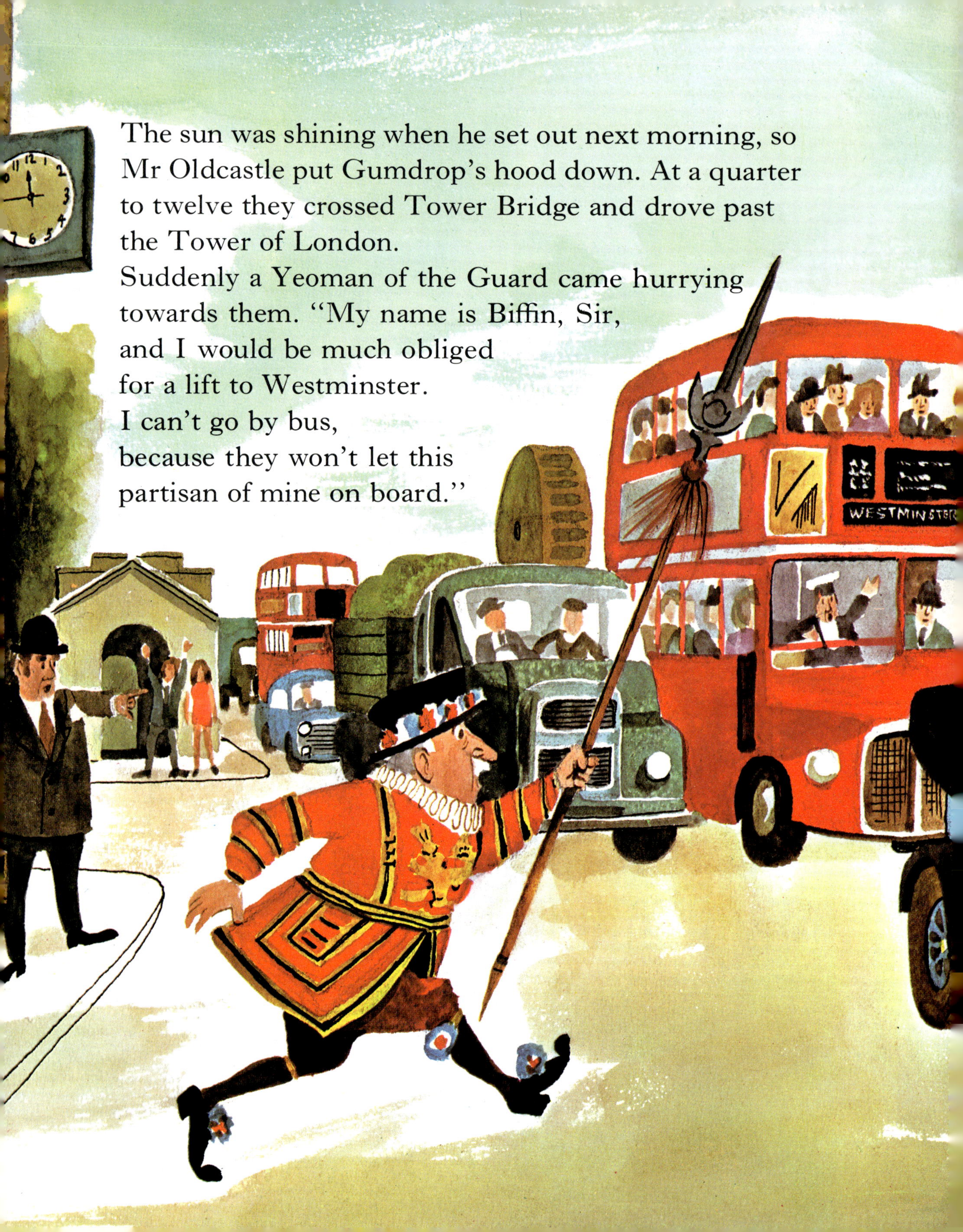

"Jump in, then!"
said Mr Oldcastle
and the grateful
beefeater, holding the
awkward weapon above
his head, did just that.

It was a quarter past twelve when they reached St Paul's Cathedral. Just then two men ran out of a building, jumped into a small yellow car, turned sharply into the road so that Gumdrop had to stop, and drove smartly away.

"Stop those men!" shouted a policeman who ran out of the building too and jumped into Gumdrop. "I am Sergeant Bluemantle and I was called to apprehend those persons who have just stolen five thousand pounds from the Bank. We must catch them, so please be good enough to drive as fast as you can after them!"

And Mr Oldcastle did just that.

There was heavy traffic in Fleet Street and the going was slow. The yellow car was way ahead of them. It was nearly a quarter to one by the time they reached the Law Courts, where they had to stop again.

A man in a wig was sitting in the middle of a zebra crossing, and he was very angry.

"Those uncouth villains in that impossible yellow contraption have just knocked me down! If I don't see them prosecuted for this, then my name is not Sir Pomeroy Pendlebury-Clutterbuck, Justice of Her Majesty's High Court!"

"Please get in, then," said Mr Oldcastle, and the judge did just that.

It was a quarter past one when the bandits reached Whitehall. There they suddenly turned right, drove through a gateway and disappeared.

"Follow them through the Horseguards!" ordered Sir Pomeroy. "And you, my men," calling the two mounted sentries, "follow us!" Corporal Withers and Trooper Gaskin did just that.

It was half past one when they reached Buckingham Palace. The bandits drove their car recklessly through the band of

the Grenadier Guards, skidded round the
Victoria Memorial and roared up
Constitution Hill.
Gumdrop was stopped by Drummer Thumpit.
"I'll make mincemeat of them for this!"
he cried and jumped in. "After them!"
And Gumdrop did just that.

But the bandits were too fast for them. Gumdrop pursued them back to Piccadilly Circus and Trafalgar Square. "I shall be late for the programme on television if this goes on much longer," complained Mr Oldcastle, driving as fast as he could through the traffic-jams. "Yes, but we must arrest those fellows first!" said Sergeant Bluemantle.

"And have them up in Court," added Sir Pomeroy, "so hurry up, man!" And Mr Oldcastle did just that.

In Parliament Square Big Ben struck two and the bells of Westminster Abbey joined in. It was getting very late.

By now the yellow car was out of sight. Gumdrop couldn't go very fast because the weight of Mr Oldcastle, Beefeater Biffin, Sergeant Bluemantle, Sir Pomeroy Pendlebury-Clutterbuck and Drummer Thumpit had slowed him down considerably. It was just as well that Corporal Withers and Trooper Gaskin had their horses to ride on.

"They went up that street there!" said Lance-Corporal Albert Gunner, a Chelsea Pensioner, when they stopped to ask him.
"Get in, then," said Mr Oldcastle, "and show us the way."
And Lance-Corporal Gunner did just that.

It was nearly half past two when they reached the Albert Hall, and it was getting extremely late. But they had to stop again to allow members of the Philharmonic Orchestra to cross over from the Albert Memorial.

"If you are chasing that yellow menace that nearly had us over just now then I will come and show you which way they went," cried Mr Owen Llewellyn the trombone player. "Indeed to goodness I will!" And he did just that.

"I shall NEVER get to Television Centre at this rate!" protested Mr Oldcastle. He drove on as fast as he could until they came to Shepherd's Bush.

"There they go!" cried all the passengers in Gumdrop. "We'll catch them yet!" But the yellow car was too fast for them again. It roared up a straight road. It was almost out of sight when, suddenly, the bandits saw a police car in the road. They turned their car sharply and drove through an open gate. Gumdrop went after them and the police car followed behind.

"Look there!" cried Mr Oldcastle in delight. "They've brought us to where I have been trying to drive all day!" For it was the BBC Television Centre, and it was five minutes to three.

BBC TELEVISION CENTRE

There was no way out for the bandits. They stopped their car, jumped out, and ran up the stairs and through the doors. Gumdrop stopped too. The passengers jumped out of Gumdrop. The policemen jumped out of the police car, and they all ran up the stairs and through the doors after the bandits.

"They might get out through the back and escape!" said Sergeant Bluemantle to Mr Oldcastle. "Let's try to head them off, then!" said Mr Oldcastle. He turned Gumdrop round and did just that.

He drove Gumdrop through a wide doorway into a curved corridor which ran round the whole building. They turned a corner and there they had to stop.

The bandits were running towards them, and all the others chasing the bandits were running too. Gumdrop was blocking the way, so the bandits opened a door and ran straight in.

It was the television studio and the time was three o'clock.

In the studio the programme had just started. Everybody else came tumbling in after the bandits. The television cameras were working as the bandits were surrounded. They were held fast by the policemen from the police car as Sergeant Bluemantle handcuffed the robbers.

So ended Gumdrop's journey to London. It had turned into a wild chase through London after two desperate bank robbers, and Mr Oldcastle had nearly missed his programme on television. But he didn't after all: instead he helped to arrest the criminals in front of the television cameras. And three million people who watched the programme saw him do it.

"This is all thanks to Gumdrop!" said the presenter of the programme to his huge audience, as Gumdrop was pushed into the studio. The cameras were still working away. "So join us now in a song to celebrate Gumdrop, that astonishing and exceptional Austin Clifton Heavy Twelve-Four, vintage 1926!"

And all the people in the studio gathered round the television camera, and all the people watching the programme gathered round their sets, and they all sang this special song for Gumdrop:

The Gumdrop Song
Oom-pa-pah, oom-pa-pah, oom-pa-oom-pa-oom-pa-pah, it's GUM-DROP —— with his
pop-pop-pop, the fin-est mo-tor car we've ev-er seen, oh
GUM-DROP, we're so glad you stopped, Every-body's looked inside,
Every-body wants a ride in old pop- pop GUM-DROP! ——
4

VETERAN

Any motor vehicle built before the end of 1904.
This is a 1903 Thornycroft two-seater

EDWARDIAN

Any motor vehicle built between 1905 and 1918.
This is a 1909 Commer 22 hp 10-seater private omnibus

VINTAGE

Any motor vehicle built between 1919 and the end of 1930. This is a 1926 Austin Heavy 12/4 Clifton 4/5-seater tourer, commonly known as Gumdrop

The Brighton Run is organised each year to commemorate the emancipation of the motor car in 1896, when the first London to Brighton Run was held. It is a strict and immutable rule now that only those cars which were built before the end of 1904 can take part. This date remains constant.

B 1628
OB 1700
F1254

GUMDROP ON THE BRIGHTON RUN

Story and pictures by Val Biro

On a sunny Sunday morning in early November only a few cars could be seen at Hyde Park Corner in London. But one was a most extraordinary car indeed: it had a blue body, black wings, brass radiator and a curly horn. It was an Austin Clifton Heavy Twelve-Four, vintage 1926, and it was called Gumdrop.

This was the day of the famous Annual Brighton Run for Veteran Cars, and Mr Josiah Oldcastle was driving Gumdrop to join them on his first Run. ''It will be grand to drive to Brighton'', he said to his dog Horace, ''and lots of people will admire Gumdrop. What's more, we might even appear on television!''
Horace gave a happy bark.

The veteran cars were already lined up in the Park when Gumdrop arrived. Lots of people admired them. But strange to say hardly anyone looked at Gumdrop. Mr Oldcastle could not understand this until the Secretary of the Club came up and spoke sternly. "Sir, your car is not old enough to join the Brighton Run."

"It is a strict rule", he went on, "that no car which was made after 1904 can take part. Gumdrop here was made in 1926, so he is only a vintage car. He is not a proper veteran."

Not old enough! Mr Oldcastle was vastly disappointed as he watched the veterans drive off. "No Brighton for us", he told Horace, "no admiration and *certainly* no tv!"

Just then a yellow omnibus appeared, full of Chelsea Pensioners. "Oi! Wait for us!" shouted the driver, but Mr Oldcastle stopped him. "You can't join the Brighton Run because you aren't old enough either."

And then he had an idea.
"I'll tell you what!
We shall have our *own*
Brighton Run. And as we
are not proper veterans, we shall not go
by the Brighton road, but on side roads instead!"
The pensioners cheered, Horace barked, Mr Oldcastle
started Gumdrop's engine and they were off.

So they drove out of London and were about to turn off the Brighton road when a man stopped them. His yellow veteran car had broken down and he had to get to Brighton in time. Of course, Mr Oldcastle offered him a lift; Mr Thornycroft got into Gumdrop and they were off.

Soon they were in the country. Suddenly, at a cross-roads, they had to stop. Because there came a wheel, all by itself – and behind it came a veteran car on three wheels only, out of control – and from the opposite direction came a truck, fast!

There will be a dreadful accident!

In a flash, Mr Oldcastle knew what he had to do. He drove Gumdrop forward and stopped. The veteran car bumped into Gumdrop's big wheel and stopped too. The truck saw Gumdrop, braked, swerved and slid into a ditch. Phew! A dreadful accident was avoided.

Boofy Greenhorn of the truck was grateful as Gumdrop pulled it out of the ditch. "There's a bit of luck!" he said. "We were hurrying to film the Brighton Run for tv tonight and thought we'd missed them."

"But we are not the proper veteran—" began Mr Oldcastle, but Boofy interrupted. "You are old crocks, aren't you? We are supposed to film the old bangers, and film you we shall." And he ran back to his truck. "My word," thought Mr Oldcastle, "Gumdrop is going to Brighton after all, and it looks as though he'll be filmed for tv too!"

After some miles, they saw a strange bicycle. "That's old Dusty Miller on his penny-farthing!" exclaimed one of the pensioners. "Come and join our Brighton Run."
After a few more miles, Horace jumped out of Gumdrop and dashed round a corner. There was another cocker spaniel called Max sitting there, in a steamroller. "You must come with us to Brighton," said Mr Oldcastle to its driver, "so that Horace can talk to your dog."

After another mile, they saw a Model-A. "Hey there, Lofty!" called Boofy to his friend, "your scrapheap is worthy of this odd lot of bangers here – come with us to Brighton."

So there was quite a cavalcade following Gumdrop now: the omnibus, the veteran, the tv truck, a steamroller, the Model-A and a penny-farthing. And Boofy filmed them all – he still thought he was filming the real Brighton Run.

At a cross-roads they stopped to let a lorry go past. "Jumping Jehosephat!" exclaimed Mr Thornycroft. "That's *my* car on that lorry there. It's been stolen. We must catch the blighters!"

T1

So Gumdrop gave chase and they soon overtook the lorry.
But they couldn't stop it. Just then, Mr Oldcastle
saw a crane at the side of the road.

"That's a stolen car back on that lorry there!" he shouted. "Get DOWN to it!" The crane-driver knew what to do: he lowered his big hook, and just as the thieves passed under it, the hook caught the Thornycroft car and lifted it straight out of the lorry. The thieves were frightened, their lorry overtook Gumdrop and they soon disappeared round the corner.

"A thousand thanks!" said Mr Thornycroft to the crane-driver. "Would you be so kind and follow us to Brighton, and bring my car?" So the crane turned and followed the procession. And all the time, Boofy filmed the scene and cried "fantastic!"

They were approaching Brighton now, downhill and going fast. Suddenly there was a cry behind Gumdrop. "Go faster! My brakes are bust!" Mr Oldcastle didn't fancy a 22 horse-power omnibus running into Gumdrop, so he went faster still. And then he saw the Brighton road ahead, and all the veteran cars coming along it!

There was only one thing to do. He slowed down. The omnibus bumped gently into Gumdrop's back. Gumdrop was pushed forward again but Mr Oldcastle jammed on the brakes. And he pulled on the handbrake, hard.

And then they stopped, just in the nick of time. Phew!
Another dreadful accident was avoided.

It was a great moment when they arrived in Brighton, with all the people cheering Gumdrop and his strange procession as they came in, ahead of the proper veterans of the real Brighton Run.

So they *did* come to Brighton and they *were* cheered by all and they *would* appear on television after all!

When they finally stopped, the Secretary of the Club came up. "Thank you for bringing our President to Brighton in time," he said. "And I thank you," said the President, who was none other than Mr Thornycroft, "for saving the day. To acknowledge our gratitude to you and your splendid vehicle, I hereby elect Gumdrop as an Honorary Veteran Car Extraordinary, so that you can join the Brighton Run every year from now on!"

And the twenty million people who watched Boofy's film that night on television did not seem to notice that they watched the wrong Brighton Run. They thought what an exciting Brighton Run this GUMDROP Run had been!

They watched

How Gumdrop saved the three-wheeled veteran

How Gumdrop pulled out the tv truck

How they chased the thieves

How the crane saved the stolen car

How Gumdrop stopped the omnibus

And how all the people cheered Gumdrop at the end of it all.

Mildew Manor
Showing the Ancestral and HAUNTED Home of Sir Marmaduke Ricketty-Cobwebb, on the Day of GUMDROP's Visit

For Mimi – without whose ghosting this story would only be half as spooky

GUMDROP FINDS A GHOST

Story and pictures by Val Biro

ON A SUNNY MORNING in June, Mr Josiah Oldcastle twitched his floppy moustache. 'Dan,' he said to his grandson, 'let's go out today and visit Mildew Manor, the ancestral home of Sir Marmaduke Ricketty-Cobwebb. It is a very old house and who knows, we might even meet a ghost!'

Dan was not so sure about meeting ghosts because they were apt to shuffle and moan around in a most alarming way. But when he saw the bulging picnic basket he was glad; and when he heard that they would go in Gumdrop, he was delighted. He jumped into the car and announced: 'I'm ready – let's go!'

Mildew Manor was an awesome sight. You would have expected a ghost – a veritable host of ghosts – to appear out of its nooks and crannies at any moment. Dan felt a little scared at the thought.

'Don't worry,' said Mr Oldcastle, 'just hold my hand as we go round the house. If we do meet a ghost, I shall twitch my moustache and frighten it off.' So they parked Gumdrop in a safe place and joined the other visitors to the Manor.

They walked through the hall and Dan thought that the fierce-looking suits of armour might leap into life at any moment and chase all the visitors away. But they remained motionless.

In the drawing room they saw a vast fireplace and Dan thought that a ghost might slide down the chimney and begin to shuffle and moan. But there was not a sound.

They went into the State Bedroom, and Dan half expected to see a ghost stretched out in the huge four-poster. But the bed was empty.

In the Picture Gallery hung the portraits of all the Ricketty-Cobwebbs. One of them, Sir Crankshaft, had apparently been very fond of cars, but he was a bad driver and very forgetful. He went for a drive on the Estate one day and walked back without his car. He said that he had lost it – but he had forgotten where!

'Fancy losing a car!' thought Dan. Sir Crankshaft must have been a very odd old man indeed.

It was when they walked along a dark and shadowy passage that it happened. To their horror, they saw a swaying, shuffling, wavering figure gliding towards them. A ghost! It uttered strange moans and everybody shrieked and ran away as fast as they could. Dan wanted to run too. But Mr Oldcastle stood firm. He twitched his moustache. Once. Twice. Three times.

And a funny thing happened. The ghost stopped moaning and began to giggle. Then it burst into laughter, took its head off and tucked it under its arm. Its real head was still laughing. 'Foiled again!' laughed the ghost. 'If I may say so, your moustache is so amusing that I can't keep this up any longer. Allow me to introduce myself – I am Sir Marmaduke Ricketty-Cobwebb, owner of this Manor.'

Dan was greatly relieved to see that it was not a real ghost after all. 'My visitors really do want to see a ghost,' explained Sir Marmaduke as he escorted them out of the house. 'Unfortunately we haven't got one, so I have to pretend to be one myself. But it is rather wearisome to go shuffling and moaning around all day, just to keep the visitors happy. Now, if only I could find a *real* ghost, I would have a special room set aside for it with a notice saying *This Way to The Ghost*.'

They had reached the car park by now, and when Sir Marmaduke saw Gumdrop he jumped about as if *he* had seen a ghost. 'What a beautiful car!' he exclaimed. 'How my uncle Crankshaft would have loved it! How I wish that *I* owned a lovely old car like this!' Mr Oldcastle understood the feeling and suggested that Sir Marmaduke come with them in Gumdrop and share their picnic.

They drove off across the Estate and up a steep track towards a wood on top of the hill. 'This is a lovely spot,' said Sir Marmaduke, 'I haven't been here for years. Let's have our picnic.' So they stopped Gumdrop, spread a rug on the grass, and settled down. Dan climbed into Gumdrop's driving seat – his very favourite place.

After the picnic Sir Marmaduke got up. 'Do you mind if I do a spot of ghost-practising? I still have a lot to learn – not least to refrain from laughing when people twitch their moustaches at me.' So saying, he started to shuffle and glide around, uttering his strange moans – while Mr Oldcastle twitched his floppy moustache at him.

Dan found all this so funny that he laughed and jumped up and down in the driving seat. In doing so he must have kicked against Gumdrop's handbrake, because slowly the car started to move downhill!

'Stop, Dan, stop!' yelled Mr Oldcastle. 'Pull the handbrake! Press the footbrake!' Gumdrop was rolling down the track quite fast now and Dan grabbed the steering wheel. His leg was too short to reach the footbrake and he had no hand to spare for the handbrake. It was hard work steering the runaway Gumdrop on that steep track and as they reached a sharp bend, Dan was quite unable to turn the wheel quickly enough.

So Gumdrop rolled straight on, across a ditch and down towards the edge of the Estate.

Dan steered Gumdrop between some trees and bushes which helped to slow him down. It wasn't downhill any more and, with a little *bump*, Gumdrop finally stopped. He was hardly visible among the foliage.

'Where have they got to?' called Sir Marmaduke anxiously. 'I've never seen this part of the Estate before!' They searched for some time, when Mr Oldcastle discovered Gumdrop and Dan in the bushes and was much relieved to find that neither of them had come to much harm. 'Well done, my boy,' he said, 'you will make a fine driver one day! '

Dan was much relieved too, although his legs were still shaking a bit. He pushed his way through the foliage to see what Gumdrop had bumped against. He looked – then he stared – and then he shouted excitedly. 'Come and look! See what Gumdrop has found! A great big leafy mouldy mildewy muddy beautiful old car!!'

Mr Oldcastle stared too and twitched his moustache so many times that his glasses fell off. Then he started shouting. 'This is a veritable Ghost! Sir Marmaduke, come and see a Ghost!'

It was Sir Marmaduke's turn to stare and shout now. 'This must be the car which my uncle Crankshaft lost all those years ago! And your clever Gumdrop has actually found it at last!' He jumped about for joy. 'But why did you call it a ghost?' he asked when he calmed down a bit. 'Because, my dear Sir,' replied Mr Oldcastle, 'this car is a Rolls-Royce Silver Ghost!'

And so it was that Gumdrop had found a ghost for Mildew Manor, and a lovely old car for Sir Marmaduke. It is on view to this day at the Manor, beautifully repaired and polished, in a room specially set aside for it, with a notice saying

People come for miles to see this *real* and lovely ghost, and Sir Marmaduke has no need to shuffle and moan around any more.

And on warm and sunny days he asks Mr Oldcastle and Dan to come over in Gumdrop and they drive round the Estate, Gumdrop in front, the Ghost behind, to the delight of all.

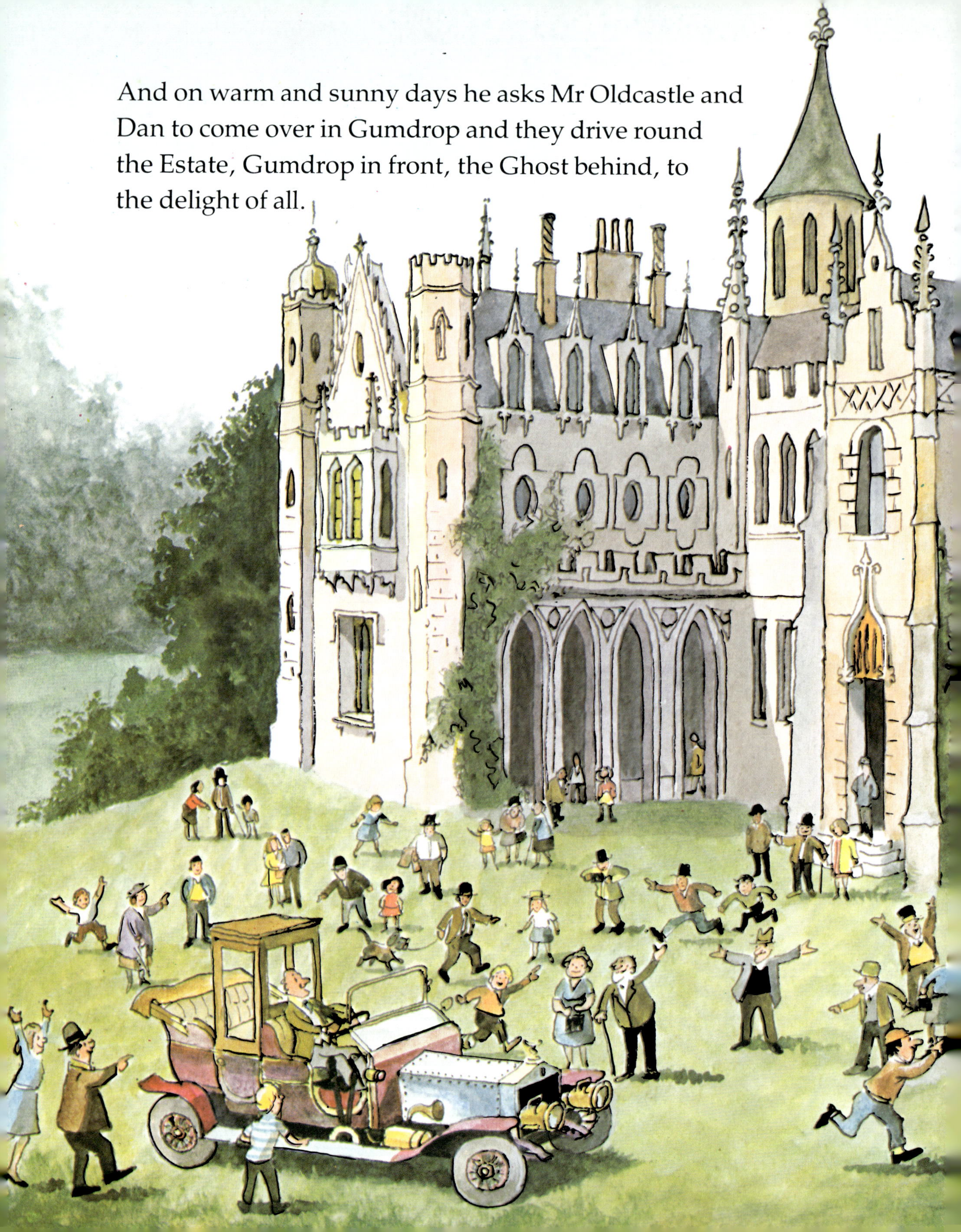

The most important peopl

nd things in this story

For Mimi
who made this story shipshape,
with love

GUMDROP AT SEA

Story and pictures by Val Biro

ON A SUNNY summer's day the road to the sea was jammed with traffic. BEEP-BEEP went the horns, and TOOTLE-TOO! People were getting impatient because something was holding them up.

HONK-HONK went another horn. It belonged to a very special car: an Austin Clifton Heavy 12/4, vintage 1926. And there is of course only one car with a horn like that. His name is Gumdrop.

Mr Josiah Oldcastle sat at the wheel and HONKed again. He was getting impatient too, and so was his dog, Horace.

He went WOOF-WOOF.

And do you know who was holding up the traffic? Why, it was the Bumblebee family. Their car had broken down, as it frequently did. And they didn't know what to do.
'The car won't go!' complained Mr Bumblebee.
'Our holiday is ruined!' wailed Mrs Bumblebee.
The Bumblebee children just moaned and demanded icecream.

'Let me help you,' said
Mr Oldcastle. He had recognised
his neighbours and he brought Gumdrop
up to give them a tow to a garage.
So they hitched the battered car to Gumdrop
while Mrs Bumblebee directed the traffic with her parasol.

As they drove to a nearby garage Gumdrop struggled under the heavy load. His engine went Brrrrm-CLANG-Brrrrm-Brrrrm-CLANG. Mr Oldcastle did not like those CLANGs.

'It is probably your
big ends going,' said the
garage man. 'Not surprising,
really, in an old car like this!'
Mr Oldcastle did not like the sound
of that at all, but they wanted to get to
the sea in time. So the Bumblebees left their
car for repairs and squeezed into Gumdrop to
continue their journey to the sea.

Gumdrop had to climb a steep hill on the way, and as he did so his engine went Brrrrm-CLANGETY-brrrrm-CLANG-CLANG. The Bumblebees were really too heavy for the old car.

'Your big end's going!' said Mr Bumblebee. 'How frightful!' cried Mrs B. 'We want icecream!' wailed the children. 'Woof-woof,' went Horace.

Mr Oldcastle said nothing because he did not like those CLANGETY-CLANGs one little bit.

At long last there was the harbour and everybody cheered up. Even Gumdrop sounded happy: Brrrrm-brrrrm went his engine as if nothing had happened. He was a reliable old car and he had brought his heavy load safely to the sea.

But just as they parked on the shore, Gumdrop's engine made the most *terrible* noises. It clanged and clattered as if it were ready to explode! And in a cloud of smoke and a final mighty BANG! it stopped.

'Oh my goodness!' exclaimed Mr Oldcastle as he looked under the bonnet. 'The engine's blown up!' There was oil everywhere and a great big hole in the crankcase.
'Oh dear!' said Mr Bumblebee. 'Your big end's gone all right! And that big hole can't be repaired, either!'

Mr Oldcastle knew that only too well. Gumdrop would need a new engine now. But where would he find another 1926 Austin 12/4 engine? He might have to search around for years!
For the moment there was nothing to be done and as the Bumblebees were impatient to go for a sail, Mr Oldcastle decided to go with them.
Poor old Gumdrop was left standing on the shore.

They hired an old fishing boat. 'All aboard!' called Mr Bumblebee who was the captain now. 'Hoist the sails! Anchors away!' And they sailed out into deep waters, with many a 'gybe-oh!' and 'ready about!'

Mrs B. lay back to sunbathe under her parasol. The children ate icecream and Horace tried to fish. Everybody was happy – except Mr Oldcastle who was thinking about Gumdrop's broken engine.

The tide was flowing and a strong wind blew up. Mr Bumblebee got out his telescope and scanned the horizon. Then he turned his gaze towards the shore. 'Look, the water is nearly up to Gumdrop!'

Mr Oldcastle was much alarmed. 'We must turn back at once,' he cried, 'or Gumdrop will be washed out to sea!' But just at that moment Horace saw a fish. He grabbed at it but unfortunately he lost his balance and . . .

SPLASH! he fell straight into the water. Mr Oldcastle was dismayed. As if he hadn't enough worries already! But he did not hesitate. He plunged into the waters there and then, to rescue his dog.

Mr Bumblebee leant over the side to help and the others grabbed Horace to pull him on board. Unfortunately, all this extra weight tilted the boat so much that . . .

with a great big SPLASH! the Bumblebees
fell into the water, too!
'Mayday! Mayday!' boomed Mr Bumblebee.
'Help!' Help!' gurgled Mrs B.
'Icecream! Icecream!' spluttered
the children. And Mr Oldcastle
saw their boat floating away
with the tide.

But soon some boats sailed up to rescue them. Everybody was hauled on board, and it was then that Mr Oldcastle remembered Gumdrop. 'Hurry, hurry!' he cried, 'or my car will be washed out to sea!'

When they reached the shore the water was already up to Gumdrop's mudguards. There was no time to lose. 'Shoulders to the wheel!' commanded Mr B. and everybody strained and heaved and pulled and pushed until Gumdrop was safely back on dry land at last.

It was then that Mr Oldcastle remembered Horace.
'My dog! Where's my dog?' he cried in anguish.
But Horace was nowhere to be seen!
Poor Mr Oldcastle! First his car blew up, then it was
nearly washed out to sea while he was almost drowned himself.
And now his dog was missing. What a day of disasters!

As he looked round he saw that their own fishing boat had floated in on the tide and stopped in front of Gumdrop. What's more, he heard a sort of muffled bark, WHOOMPH-WHOOMPH.

Mr Oldcastle leapt on board. The sound came from under the engine-cover. He tore it off – and there was Horace, sitting by the engine, safe and sound! He folded the dog in his arms and felt happy for the first time that day.

Then he looked at the boat's engine. It was old. It was big. It was beautiful. And it was exactly like Gumdrop's.

'Why, it's a genuine 1926 Austin 12/4 engine and not a crack or a hole anywhere!' Mr Oldcastle could hardly believe his good luck. Good old Horace had found the perfect engine for Gumdrop!

Mr Oldcastle danced around so joyfully that Horace got quite dizzy in his arms.

The fisherman who owned the old boat was quite happy to sell the engine.
'It came out of an old car just like yours,' he said.
'Anyway I'd just as soon have a modern Diesel for my boat.'

So all was well in the end. Mr Oldcastle took the precious engine to be overhauled and then joined the Bumblebees on their holiday. He bought icecreams for the children every day and Horace caught as much fish as he wanted.
Best of all, Gumdrop has a sparkling new engine now and he is running better than ever. What's more, Mr Oldcastle is determined to keep his car firmly on dry land from now on. Brrrrm-brrrrm!